AF234773

Table of Contents

Introduction

Data is an asset that is available to virtually every organization on the planet, it is simply a set of facts and statistics, qualitative and quantitative variables collected together for reference and analysis. Data can also be referred to as the lifeblood of every organization (computerised or manually documented) if it is allowed to flow freely across the entire ecosystem. In computing, data is information that is translated into a form that is efficient for movement or processing, it is measured, collected, reported and analysed, whereupon it can be visualised using images, videos, graphs and other tools used for analysis. Data discovery is a powerful trend causing reverberations throughout the business intelligence industry. There is a good chance that data is mentioned in almost every business meeting and these days even in friendly conversations. The world is rapidly turning into a data driven habitat just like electricity, data has become a basic enterprise asset that is quickly revolutionizing the world, enabling better, faster and cheaper business processes. The surge of data driven culture has had a significant impact on how organisations are structured, being data driven simply means making use of massive quantities of unstructured data ¬–text, image, video voice etc data can only take an organization so far but the people are the real drivers. We live in a world where data is often described as the new oil. Just as with oil, the value contained within data is universally recognized. As the seemingly relentless march of big data into so many aspects of the commercial and non-commercial world continues, the practicalities of constructing and implementing data-driven business models (DDBMs) has become an ever-more important area of study and application. In recent times companies are striving to become data- driven. But some do not know the exact meaning, More than just installing the right tools and applications, becoming data -driven is about making data and analytics part of the business strategy, its systems, processes and culture. Its about creating a mindset in which analytics form the basis of all fact-based business decisions and are embraced by all levels of the organization. With a variety of analytics tools on the market, more organizations are feeling data -savvy. Truth is, the desire to be data -driven does not equate to acting intelligently on that data. Rather, an organization must recognize the characteristics of a data- driven culture and identify opportunities to introduce relevant behaviours, in order that evidence-based decision making becomes a core part of the digital workplace. A community or company culture is built upon attitudes and beliefs that are passed down via material and habits through generations from inception. The same theory can be applied when creating a data -driven culture. The initial architecture sets the foundation for the habits and processes around the use of data. In the cause of imbibing the said process, ask yourself a real question "Is your culture well defined and framed in a way that allows employees to align with and uphold it?" For example, a low-cost provider may wish to express its culture as "we do more with less" rather than emphasize corner-cutting and belt-tightening. But this may be a culture statement that is hard for employees to rally around. Company culture should be something employees at all levels can own and exemplify — and remember that simplicity is a good thing. If employees can't articulate the culture to others in or outside the organization, they won't be able to live it. Ultimately, if you can't explicitly define your culture in a memorable way, your employees are likely to (re)define it for you.

Big data has become an invaluable tool for creating value in a business. By providing a comprehensive view of market conditions, customer needs and preferences, and potential project risks, big data can eliminate reliance on "gut feel" decision-making. Organizations can understand and embrace emerging opportunities and align products and services with changing customer needs creating additional value for stakeholders in the process. It's no news that the value of data has increased sparingly and the market capitalization of data - driven companies has grown to a higher rate than other companies in the past decade. In addition to this, the market capitalization directly impacts the EV of a company, making the company very attractive for mergers. It's not abnormal for companies to be acquired just for the data they own. IBM's acquisition of The Weather Channel is a great example of that. Now with the arrival of artificial intelligence (AI), data has become much more valuable to companies. Capitalizing on this data explosion is increasingly becoming a necessity in order for a business to remain competitive, and is a modern twist to the old adage, 'Knowledge is Power'. The challenges are threefold:

- how to extract data
- how to refine it, and
- how to ensure it is utilized most effectively.

Businesses and other organizations that fail to align themselves with data driven practices risk losing a critical competitive advantage and, ultimately, market share and the accompanying revenue.[3] for today's businesses, effective data utilization is concerned with not only competitiveness but also survival itself.

Concept of Data Driven Organisations

A data driven organisation is an organization where business decision makers are given the power to explore and access data independently, not just about seeing a few canned reports at the beginning of everyday or every week, they need to be able to ask questions and answers received based on the data before decisions are made. Firms that relentlessly measure and monitor the pulse of their businesses in continuous automated manner are also seen as data driven. A very large percentage of people want to make intelligent decisions by hard data, unfortunately in most organisations, only trained analysts and BI specialists have the power to access and manipulate complex data. The most challenging aspect of creating a data-driven organization is adjusting the culture to not just support, but also require data-centricity.

Becoming a data driven organisation must be based on the belief in the importance of the integrity and quality of information needed to permeate the culture of the organisation at all levels, also a shift in the mindset of all employees towards maintaining the integrity and quality of data is required. A data-driven organization could be described as today's Holy Grail, particularly for Chief Data Officers but also for other members of the C-Suite. By data-driven, its meant that you: consider data an input, not an output; believe data is an asset that needs to be valued, managed and protected just as its stated above; and your organization invests in and embodies being data-driven (i.e., uses data to drive decisions). In reality, the pursuit to be data-driven will require change within your organization — and, in many cases, significant change. They won't be your typical procedural changes for a specific department or team; rather, these will require changing the views and beliefs of the entire organization. Put another way: The very culture of your organization must implicitly and explicitly demand a data-centric environment. Changing an organization's culture takes time and effort. The process can be complex, and it doesn't happen by announcing, "We have a new culture." No its by implementing and acculturating that new way. It's important to first understand the role of beliefs and behaviour and how they impact culture.

A key feature of a data - driven culture is using data in a pervasive way. Data- driven companies establish processes and operations to make it easy for employees to acquire the required information, but are also transparent about data access restrictions and governance methods. These processes then impact the likelihood of enabling more mature techniques such as prescriptive analytics and creating a 360- degree view of the customer. Analytics leaders must bring in the right talent led by example and should know when not to rely on data. The assumptions, beliefs, values and behaviours of every employee make up the organization's culture, and all levels must be included in the transformational efforts. Whether explicitly defining culture through values and mission statements or allowing implied culture to prevail, all companies eventually learn that creating or changing cultural elements are difficult to control. In any decision -making process, data is a key consideration and has to be treated like an organisational asset, but moral or political factors can supersede what the data shows. Alternatively, leaders can be so focused on what the data is telling them, by so doing they miss opportunities to innovate. Some CEOs claim to have been operational on the notion of data as an asset, but only a few say their companies actually treat it that way. Here are some ways you can treat data like an asset and be rest assured you'll have positive results

Exhibit example behaviour by stressing data -driven decision making
Hire data -driven people
Ensure data- driven performance reviews and goal setting.

To understand how many companies are currently using big data to measure, create and protect values across their businesses, EY commissioned new big data research from leading insight firm Nimbus Ninety. A total of 270 senior executives responded to 27 questions on all aspects of their data strategy. Around 68% of respondents are active stakeholders in big data projects, and all departmental functions and industry sectors are represented, with the majority of respondents working in finance, marketing and IT, as well as in cross-departmental management roles. The findings of EY research shows that 81% of companies understand the importance of data for improving efficiency, business performance and that most are embarking on some kind of big data strategy. Of respondents from companies with an annual turnover of more than £2billion, only3%haveno big data strategy at all. The figure rises to 14% in the £100 million to £2 billion category and to 16% for those with annual turnover under £100 million. While the vast majority have big data on their radar, however, only 3% describe their data strategy as "mature." Among companies currently working on big data projects, just 21% are in the operational phase, showing a major gulf between companies' big data ambitions and their current achievements. In practice, this means that less than a third of companies are currently harnessing big data to offer services around existing business models and, for example up sell products and services to customers, while just 8% are using big data to optimize supply chain efficiency. Other opportunities to create value are also being missed, from improved board level decision-making to improved management of working capital. The research sheds new light on the drivers for big data adoption. "Understanding customers better" was the most common driver for big data projects, cited by 73% of respondents as a key area where additional value could be created. "Improving products and services "came close second, while almost half of respondents also cited "Improving the management of existing data" as a key focus.35%of respondents recognize the financial value of big data, citing "to monetize existing data" as a key driver. 10% were more blatant in their intention to "sort data so it can be sold to or used in partnership with a third party."20% are using data "to improve the detection and prevention of fraud", an increase from "7% of respondents who are aware of any specific data technologies as cited in our EY, Forensic Data Analytics Survey 2013."

The findings of the research suggest widespread underinvestment in the structures, processes and controls needed to support value-driven decision- making. Poor data quality and a lack of strong data governance are undermining trust in the value of data across entire organizations, while the widespread lack of specialist big data skills makes it difficult to budget and plan for big data projects and effectively calculate ROI.32% of respondents admitted to being overwhelmed by data.33% saw organizational Structure as being the key influence on success for big data projects.47% cite- "adapting organizational culture to integrate big data" as a key challenge.50%view poor data quality as a key concern, with the same percentage quoting ROI as a key challenge to projects.

Compliance is a major challenge for most businesses, despite their best intentions; many organizations will find it challenging to comply with the new regulations. For example, having multiple data bases and IT systems spread across a vast array of supplier ecosystems often makes it difficult to simply erase a customer's records, and the use of cloud-based infrastructure may lead to storage of data outside required jurisdiction. As an additional challenge, a growing landscape of cyber security threats means that organizations should expect a data breach at some time, and implement measures to limit the negative impacts, focusing more on resilience and brand damage limitation than simply trying to prevent an incident in the first place. The problem is that while companies have raced ahead with digital business strategies, effective governance and risk mitigation are often not yet in place. This largely explains why the regulator has stepped in, and why companies can no longer ignore their digital governance challenges. So what can companies do to mitigate cyber security risks and ensure that their customers 'data is kept private at all times? For many companies, the answer is the appointment of a chief data officer (CDO) with end to-end responsibility for data governance, data management, data exploitation and data security. The CDO's remit covers a range of risk mitigation activities, from stress testing compliance policies and shutting down security gaps, to reassuring CEOs and regulators that adequate protection is in place for sensitive operational and customer data. Whether companies decide to appoint a CDO or not, many are reviewing their current operating models and defining data ownership, governance and management responsibilities across their businesses. In addition, companies are looking at how disruptive technologies such as cloud computing and big data are affecting their data security policies, and mapping the flow of data around their organizations to ensure compliance with jurisdictional and data management regulations. Whether a CDO is appointed or not, new roles will be required by the legislation as all companies processing more than 5,000 personal records per annum will be required to appoint a Data Protection Officer (DPO) reporting to the management board to govern compliance with the EU General Data

Privacy Regulation. Bupa and big data helping patients live longer, happier lives leading international health care group Bupa provides a broad range of healthcare services, support and advice to help people live longer, healthier, happier lives. The organization runs care homes, health centres, dental centres and hospitals, as well as providing personal and company health insurance, home health care services, health assessments and chronic disease management services. As well as serving 22 million customers in 190 countries, Bupa also provides a range of health services and advice that anyone can access. For several years, Bupa has been looking at how data can support its mission and positively influence people's health. Barry Panayi, Bupa's Head of Data Science, says, "We have amazing data resources at Bupa, but in the past they were all sitting in different areas of the business, with no real incentive for people to do anything with them. We needed to get all areas of the business involved to harness the data and use it for the benefit of our patients and the general public."The first step was to establish a group-wide community where physicians, administrators and technical staff from across Bupa could share ideas on using data to improve patient care. "We created a data group on our internal social media platform and there were 300 members within a year," says Panayi. "Managers, doctors, nursing staff and administrators were soon getting in touch to tell us how data in their areas of the organization could help improve outcomes for patients."Based on input from people in all areas of Bupa, the data science team has been able to deliver big data projects that directly benefit patients. "We have been able to compare medical outcomes across multiple physicians and facilities around the world, helping us make better decisions about where and how patients should be treated," says Panayi. "We have also looked at the cost and performance of medical supplies, including prostheses of all kinds, to improve value for patients and ensure that their treatments are successful." In one example of a recent big data project, staff in Bupa nursing homes is working with the data science team to improve care for Elderly patients suffering from dementia. "Nurses in one of our care homes noticed that patients with advanced dementia typically display repeated behaviours, such as opening and closing windows, and they need staff interventions to improve their situation," says Panayi. "Working with nursing teams, we have developed a solution that uses under-floor pressure pads and pattern recognition software to generate vast quantities of data. This can be analyzed to identify repeated behaviours and to make sure patients get the help they need."When Bupa updated their award winning rehabilitation programme on behalf of the National Health Service for people suffering with the severe lung condition COPD, big data was able to improve medical outcomes. Alan Payne, Bupa's Corporate Digital Director, says, "We gave nurses tablets, where they could enter patient information and test results directly into a clinical grade database, rather than just making notes. By analyzing data on patients' capabilities and breathing, we were able to focus on the types of exercises that would be most beneficial for them."Using accurate patient data, it was possible to design effective outcome-based regimens for 2,600 people attending the pilot rehabilitation course. "On average, the prescribed exercises helped patients reduce their oxygen use by 1.5 litres per day during the course, representing a potential, NHS-wide cost saving of £115 million a year," says Alan. "More importantly, the data showed that the Bupa rehabilitation course can help to improve the physical capabilities and quality of life for COPD sufferers."While the benefits of Bupa's big data initiatives are profound, Panayi says consent is critical before any patient data is used. "Patients must trust us to make the best health care decisions on their behalf, but they must also trust that their personal data is being protected and used appropriately," he says. "That's why we've built patient consent into every one of our big data initiatives, and why we explain to patients exactly how the data will help them overcome their health challenges." Panayi likens it to a contract: "Our patients agree to give us their valuable data, and we agree to use it in their best interests to positively influence their health," he says. The data science team stresses that patients — not technology — are at the heart of Bupa's big data initiatives. "Through our online community and working group, we identify issues and patient needs first and discover where data and technology can add value for them," he says. "We see ourselves as health care providers first and data scientists second, and we are very proud of the contribution we are making to helping patients live longer, healthier, happier lives. "This research shows that, EY has developed a big data capability framework. This outlines the components needed to support value-driven decisions, including centralized governance and technology infrastructure. It also shows how strategy and specific big data functionality combine to support value-based decision-making. By proposing a best practice model for big data, the big data capability map helps big data teams demonstrate the potential for value creation among senior level managers.

The value framework enables us to choose the appropriate type of analytics for the challenge. Do you need to know the next best action, or do you need to know why something is happening? Do you need to do this repeatedly or is it a one off question? By being clear about the type of analytics required, this will help focus on the right tools, skill sets and solutions. The main reason organizations struggle with data quality is because there is neither ownership nor accountability for quality. Many organizations are now focusing their offering behind the chief data officer and ensuring that data is seen as an asset equal to others. The visible protection of data is critical to retain customers, employees and suppliers trust. It is fundamental to have access to this data, and not being able to prove to these stakeholder groups that you can protect their data will place you at a competitive disadvantage. Our research shows that while almost all businesses now recognize the power of analytics to grow, optimize and protect value, many continue to be overwhelmed by the far-reaching changes required to transition to value driven decision making. Lack of strong leadership and limited investment are hindering companies at every stage of the big data journey, from building a credible business case to ROI modelling, capability development, project planning and project delivery. This, in turn, is undermining the potential for measuring existing value, creating additional value and protecting value that already exists in an organization. Becoming an analytics-driven organization to create value becoming a true value driven organization "Analytics is changing how organizations make decisions and take actions. Data by itself has limited value but when managed as a strategic asset, data can change how organizations compete and win." The new marketing mantra says, "Know your consumer and use this knowledge for good". It sounds as easy as that. However, there is a trick. We all understand that shoppers are getting smarter and increasingly less predictable - they use multiple channels throughout their shopping journey; they get information about the product from different sources, they may never even visit your shop in reality before making a purchase. You may never even see your real customer's face- to-face, getting that "consumer data" has never been more challenging. Your customers expect you to know who they are, what keeps them up at night, what time they have breakfast at, and which brand of soda they refer. Ok, that' s a bit of exaggeration here, but it' s true that consumers expect timely and relevant messages from marketers , otherwise they tag that ad , email or newsletter as "spam" and get rid of it without a single drop of remorse. And if they dump you once, don't even hope they will give you a second chance later. So, one conclusion to be made here: without a 360-degree view of your audience and precise analytics based on insights gathered both online and offline, don't even try to bother those people with your ads. For this reason, using data to shape a marketing campaign is not just a passing trend. Data- driven marketing is simply how it' s going to be from now on, just get used to it. It' s been an agreement among marketers worldwide that data not only matters, but it's considered to be the most precious asset of any organization, regardless of the industry or sector .

Pitfalls and Blessings of Data-Driven Marketing
It may seem as though most marketers have a love/hate relationship with data because it's not merely the dizzying increase in the volume of data, but also the confusion about how to analyze it properly and how to put it into action. Companies are receiving different types of information about their consumers at soaring rates, but the volume is not the only issue.

Marketers have to tame customer data and analyze it rapidly to create personally tailored marketing messages for the best possible customer experience. Another challenge is the number of channels. It may be possible that a customer hits 10 or more touch points before converting. A Distinguished engineer and Sr. Director at Google, Sagnik Nandy pointed "it's challenging to be in control of your data universe because there's so much happening. There are millions of pieces of data floating around "and he was right. Combining all that information and following a consumer and adding value to each step is difficult, if not unattainable at all. Even though, if the customer journey was mapped and an attribution model was appointed, there is still a lack of data quality and completeness. Sometimes online conversions and purchases come through partner channels, such as digital networks and exchanges, which do not disclose attribution data to their members. It may be possible that a marketing team has all of the views and click data at its disposal; it may still be unclear which advertising platform brings the most profit to the business. Finally, marketers are freaking out when it comes to collecting offline data, which is more pain than gain. Worth mentioning that some organizations are still suffering from the "information silos" when a database of one department is not integrated or incompatible with a data of the other department across the organization. This leads to a lack of unified view of the information, which prevents a company from making accurate decisions. Meanwhile, other corporations lack senior management involvement when it comes to exploiting the right data and uncovering insights.

Delivering Actionable Insight to all Decision-Makers Across an Organization

To adopt the data-centric culture required to effectively find, measure and create value, organizations must be able to share actionable insight with decision makers at all levels of the business. However, EY research shows that current approaches to data collection and management make this a major challenge, largely due to widespread concerns about data quality and consistency. Specifically, data quality is cited as a challenge by 50% of companies, making it the top big data issue along with "measuring ROI on big data projects." Lack of consistency in underlying data comes third on the list, cited as a key challenge by 46% of companies. Our research shows that most companies are currently working with limited data sets for their big data projects. Half of respondents said they use data from back office systems such as enterprise resource planning (ERP), and the same percentage use data from their customer relationship management (CRM) systems, suggesting that user experience improvements and customer insight are high on their priority lists. So far, however, newer forms of data that can drive additional value creation are largely being overlooked. Only

19% are using third-party data, 29% are using data from social networks and 19% are using machine-generated data, location/spatial data, and data from communications systems such as email and messaging apps. With the right organizational structures, skills and data governance in place, organizations will be able to extend the data sets they use in the future and build a more successful data strategy that is trusted, valued and supported by key stakeholders. Using all available data to support decision-makers developing the talent needed to convert data into business value. Specialist skills are needed to develop a compelling business case for big data projects and to plan and execute them cost effectively. However, a lack of skills was the fifth most commonly cited main barrier to big data projects. While some companies lack the skills required to adopt value driven decision-making, the vast majority still rely on in-house teams to identify business requirements for big data projects, develop business cases, conduct ROI modelling and deliver projects. In an attempt to bridge the skills gap, 38% of companies are looking to hire people with big data skills, while 21% are retraining their existing technical staff. As an additional concern, only 26% of organizations are training business staff in big data-related disciplines. This shows that companies are still unprepared to adopt big data across their organizations, limiting the potential to create additional business value. Our research shows that the lack of big data skills in most companies creates significant technology challenges. For example, 36% of respondents cite "identifying big data technologies" as a challenge, and 32% report issues with technology implementation. This is not surprising given the pace of big data technology developments To overcome these challenges and maximize the potential for value creation, organizations must acquire the skills needed to deliver every stage of a big data project, from building an effective business case and modelling ROI, to selecting and implementing a successful technology strategy and appropriate, cost-effective architectures. These can be achieved by bringing new skills on board and changing the organizational structure to embed big data into the decision-making processes. Another useful strategy is to partner with third-party companies who are big data specialists, including consultancies, boutique big data providers, systems integrators and software-as-a service providers. While big data skills are needed to overcome technology challenges, there is some good news for smaller companies wishing to embrace value-driven decision making. With only a 9% gap between big data activities in small and large companies, we are seeing a democratization of advanced analytics through developments such as pay as-you go cloud computing and software as-a-service. Keeping up with technology remains a challenge.

Steps to Becoming a Data-Driven Organization

Becoming a data-driven organization requires a change to your culture, beliefs and behavioural pattern of every employee. This five-step process to structure your communication focuses on the importance of inspiring beliefs and behaviours and how to use them to support changes you need to make: This process should align with the scope and priorities of your program. And although your vision, purpose and picture may appear lofty, aspiration and broad, your plan and who is participating will be more specific and tactical.

Vision - a high-level strategic statement of your goal.

Purpose - why you are executing the vision.

Picture - what future state looks like and the principles for attaining it.

Plan - how and when you will get to the desired future state.

Participation - who is responsible for the needed changes.

VISION

Before you move into implementation planning, it is important to create a unified vision or statement of your organization's goal. Your vision statement should represent the desired future state of your organization and should:

- Be specific and direct
- Inspire beliefs to direct behaviours
- Be high-level in its strategic reach

  Consider this framework for a vision statement, which is specific and direct — yet still high-level: Completed, the vision statement should be succint and evoke your broader company culture and be benefits-oriented; for example: AcmeTech's new Data Governance program shores up internal procedures and practices that will reduce costs from bad data and the related error correction payments, saving the company millions. Once you establish your information management program's vision statement, it will become a touch stone for inspiring your organization to become data-driven.

PURPOSE

Next, think about the "why" for your vision statement — the purpose for the goal. Why is it important for your organization to achieve it? The answer will be personal and unique to your organization and will be broad or specific depending on your current scope. Here are some to get you started:

It will simplify and improve our quarter-end closing process, which saves us time, money and frustration.

It will enhance our customer experience, which will lead to less churn and higher customer lifetime value.

It will make our product line more complete, which makes us more competitive.

It will complement our digital strategy, which is critical to the growth and long-term success of the organization.

Some purposes — such as "It will comply with legislative requirements, which keeps regulators out of our business" — are inherently less motivational. But it is important to express the beliefs associated with them, because when vision and purpose are aligned, they power you through other steps in this process. The vision needs to be communicated continuously and consistently across the organization. Everyone in the organization, from business users to IT developers, needs to understand why the change is happening, what impact it will have on their teams and where are they going with it. If employees understand and believe in the vision, the organization as a whole will be motivated and will strive for the change, ultimately creating more change agents.

PICTURE

Vision and purpose are often not enough to inspire alignment within an organization. Employees need to picture what the goal-state will look like in order to support and participate in the change. One way to fully conceptualize the outcome of a change is by contrasting it to the current state. Use specific examples of what will be changing to deepen and strengthen your vision and purpose:

- Before - Our data is often a burden, with its inherent   issues and challenges.
- Now - Our data is a key competitive asset, now that we understand and trust it.
- Before - Data is our customer, vendor and product information.
- Now - Data is a critical, corporate asset, and I see how it enables decisions to drive growth.

A guiding principle is another way for employees to picture the organization's values through a statement of expected behaviour. This example states the behavioural aspects succinctly, followed by further explanation, while supporting the vision and purpose: We are accountable for the data we produce. As individuals, we create new data every day. We must make sure it is of the highest quality by following agreed-upon standards and guidelines. This will allow everyone in our organization to trust the data we use.

PLAN

Your vision, purpose and picture will only take you so far; you need a plan to get your organization to its desired future state. It should include details and an implementation timeline that lets employees know when they will receive the information, training and support them need to make the transition. At a minimum, the plan should include information about:

What changes are needed (how they support future state)
What EIM will facilitate (key steps and milestones?)
The enterprise roadmap (a big-picture view)
Group-specific roadmaps (collaboration that is required).

It is important for managers to understand how their own work will change over time, as well as how their employees' work changes. Remember to communicate the plan to managers in advance, so they are able to be evangelize and support your company-wide messages. It's important to define a forward-looking data -driven strategy using clear and concise language. This vision creates a platform that helps the organization work toward a common goal and the framework against which it can begin to develop a strategy. When properly developed and presented, the strategy can help bolster credibility and encourage more leaders to join the coalition, particularly those with any doubts regarding the mission. A typical strategy would use a phased approach, with interim goals and milestones defined. One example of creating a data drive strategy is to create a data centre of excellence. This team would handle all data governance, data integration, and analytics initiatives.

PARTICIPATION
Achieving a data-driven company requires the coordination and collaboration of every employee, team and group across the organization. For the vision to be realized and the plan to be implemented, clear roles and responsibilities are key — so, too, is communicating how individuals and/or groups will work together.
Questions to clarify about participation include:

- What is my specific role, and how will my job change?
- Who does what on my team and/or in the groups with whom we interact?
- What are the related responsibilities across the enterprise?

What are the assignments specifically within EIM?

When you are specific about what participation is needed and by whom, this collectively helps to move everyone forward.

DATA DRIVEN BUSINESS MODELS

The research suggests that many businesses are developing new business models specifically designed to create additional business value by extracting, refining and ultimately capitalizing on Data. Such innovation is notoriously difficult – particularly for large existing firms who have to contend with ingrained company structure, culture and traditional revenue streams. It is the Competitive advantage associated with effective big data utilization that is driving the desire for existing mainstream businesses to become data-driven. The DDBM blueprint presented within this article is an academically secured and industry-focused data innovation platform, which organizations desiring to become data-driven or facing difficulties with data-use innovation can utilize to help construct their own DDBM. Data-driven businesses have been demonstrated to have an output and productivity that is 5–6 percent higher than similar organizations who are not utilizing data-driven processes. In some industries, such as publishing, big data has spawned entirely new business models. For example, after a movement towards a digitally oriented distribution model and dwindling advertising revenues, certain publishers began to accumulate data relating to their online users – users whose demographic was particularly attractive to advertisers. This data could then be sold, enabling targeted and more effective advertising. In the financial services sector trading algorithms analyze huge quantities and varieties of data, enabling the capture of value in milliseconds. It is unsurprising that 71 per cent of 2banking firms directly report that the use of big data provides them with a competitive advantage –each often finding a slightly different angle to the data application. Clearly there is value associated with effective big data utilization, and the race is on for existing businesses, both large and small, to capitalize upon it. However, although big-data-oriented publications agree on the potentially positive impact of big data utilization, very few suggest how, in practice, it can be attained and none offer a research-based guide or blueprint that can be utilized by an existing business to help create and implement its own DDBM. An example of this is a recent article published in the Harvard Business Review, which provides five new patterns of innovation, three of which relate directly to data and its derivable benefits.

While these patterns are identified in the article, there is no systematic framework proposed to enable established organizations and business start-ups to transform an innovative data-driven idea into a feasible

DDBM. This article aims to address this apparent void by providing a foundation and structural guidelines within which an existing or new business can analyze, construct and apply its own DDBM. This can be achieved ab initio or with inspiration from existing DDBM examples, the latter allowing an organization to benefit from proven policies in similar organizations that have been successful with DDBM implementation. We also argue that creating a business model for a data-driven business involves answering six fundamental questions:

What do we want to achieve by using big data?

What is our desired offering?

What data do we require and how are we going to acquire it?

In what ways are we going to process and apply this data?

How are we going to monetize it?

What are the barriers to us accomplishing our goal?

In order to create a blueprint that could be an effective guide for existing businesses to create and implement their own DDBMs, it was important to identify the main constituents and operation of DDBMs currently applied in both business start-ups and established businesses. The organizations analyzed were chosen randomly through literature reference frequency using a number generator method that utilizes background radiation to achieve randomness. Established businesses were chosen from five sectors (finance, insurance, publishing, retail, telecoms), which were determined through big data literature reference frequency.

These sectors were then searched for on Google and the first 20 distinct businesses were pulled from the list. This left four organizations for each of the five sectors. Furthermore, samples of 100 business start-ups were taken from the start-up incubator AngelList. The start-up sample was limited to companies from the category 'big data' or 'big data analytics'. For the purpose of this article, a random number generator was used to choose 40 random organizations from both start-ups and established businesses to demonstrate how these organizations utilize and construct their own DDBMs using the six proposed questions. For each of the chosen business organizations publicly available documents were collected and consisted primarily of annual reports, website information and business-school case studies. Specific news articles were also obtained from financial, market and business-oriented publications such as Financial Times of London, The Wall Street Journal and The New York Times. In total, over two hundred sources were collected. A thematic language analysis was then conducted using the analytics software Nvivo. Each document was manually coded towards a framework developed by Hartmann et al. (2014), derived from academic literature. This process gradually deciphered the DDBM of each Individual business while developing the more generalized DDBMs for established businesses and business start-ups. Validation of the thematic language analysis was achieved through qualitative research that is twofold: first, by interviews, and second, through the use of a survey – both of which were aimed at strategy and data-oriented representatives within each of the businesses. Finally, company-specific case studies were formulated as a means for further validation.

What do we want to achieve by using big data?

In order for a business to effectively utilize big data it is vital that its aims are clear and realistically attainable. Often an organization understands the potential value and benefit associated with data but fails to determine a specific aim before undertaking a time-consuming and costly data acquisition and analysis process. By targeting a pre-determined outcome the business can retain its focus on a desired and realistic goal and reduce unnecessary monetary and human resource wastage during the process. Our analysis shows the following seven key competitive advantages identified by our selected business organizations; shortened supply chain, expansion, consolidation, processing speed, differentiation and brand. Brand was considered to be the most important competitive advantage to established organizations, with 95 per cent of analyzed companies regarding it as a competitive advantage. This was followed closely by differentiation (90%) and expansion (70%). Shortened supply chain and processing speed were considered less significant to the established organizations we analyzed, ranging from 20 to 30 per cent of organizations regarding these as a competitive advantage. As Figure 2 shows, brand is considered the most important competitive advantage throughout all of the sectors analyzed. Differentiation is seen as important in retail, publishing and insurance. Processing speed is considered a strong advantage by the finance sector. The fashion retailer Zara aimed to achieve close to real-time customer insight into fashion industry trends and purchasing patterns so that it could better align itself with its customers, resulting in increased retail sales volume. Zara knew it wanted to utilize a shortened supply chain to gain competitive advantage and to structure its resources efficiently and effectively. By incorporating near real-time sales statistics, blog posts and social media data into its analytic systems, Zara is able to rush emerging trends to market. One example was the social media 'storm', which occurred over a dress worn by the female musician Beyoncé on the opening night of her world tour. Before the culmination of the tour Zara had already designed, manufactured and begun capitalizing on this trend in its retail stores. The near real-time analysis of large volumes of unstructured data creates potential revenues that were unthinkable a decade ago. The online retailer ASOS instead aimed to develop differentiation as its desired competitive advantage.

Although the organization incorporates a similar data strategy to Zara, it produces a much higher variety of items because it is not restricted in terms of space like the typical 'bricks and mortar' stores. By utilizing an effective data strategy to keep on top of industry trends, and combining this with an extensive product range, ASOS maximizes the probability of customers finding products that they want to buy.

What is our desired offering?

A business must decide in what way the DDBM construct will benefit the company's current offering or, alternatively, create an entirely new one. Established businesses have a tendency to utilize data to improve or enhance their current customer offering, which is often called a 'value proposition'. It therefore follows that the value proposition is the value created for customers through the offering. A company can offer raw data that is primarily 'a set of facts' without an attached meaning. When data has been interpreted it becomes information or knowledge. Typically the output of any analytics activity attaches some insight or application. Organizations are not restricted to a single offering. Established organizations, in particular, tend to have multiple customer offerings. Of the established organizations analyzed 100 per cent had an offering that was a non-data product or service, 24 per cent had information and knowledge offerings and 20 per cent had data as one of their offerings. This is not surprising considering the historical context of many of these traditional organizations and the recent advances in data-oriented activities and revenue streams. The offering reference percentage for a non-data product or service in the retail and insurance sectors was 100 per cent, suggesting that accumulated data from varying sources is used internally. A non-data product or service was also the dominant offering in the publishing and finance sectors, acquiring 48 and 85 per cent respectively. Telecommunications had a strong reference percentage for data as an offering at 50 per cent. Publishing also had a strong data offering reference percentage, attaining over 35 per cent. For example, the mobile phone service provider AT&T increased the positive public perception of its brand after evaluating a customer sentiment analysis based upon both internal (current users) and external (potential users) data sources. This insight enabled AT&T to improve its product and service offering in areas considered most important to its potential and actual customers, thus maximizing the derived benefit from the investment. Furthermore, organizations have to identify with those whom these offerings should target. There are several ways to segment customers.

However, the most generic classification was used, dividing target customers into businesses (B2B), individual consumers (B2C) and consumer to consumer (C2C), which is defined as facilitating the use of customers to acquire further customers. In many cases, companies could target businesses and individual consumers. For 75 per cent of the companies analyzed, B2C was their dominant target customer. B2B customer targeting was lower, with 50 per cent of the established organizations referencing this as their target customer. The C2C business model was utilized least as a means to target new customers, with 20 per cent of the business organizations analyzed referencing this activity. In the retail and insurance sectors B2C targeting was the dominant target customer node, attaining 76 and 54 per cent of the percentage references for their sector. A B2B target customer was referenced in the publishing (61% of references) and finance (72% of references) sectors. Organizations utilizing C2C were seen in lower percentages (<20%) in the retail and publishing sectors. In the telecommunications sector C2C was the dominant target customer, with 45 percent of references. However, the majority of C2C references were related to one 6 company, GiffGaff Mobile, whose innovative business model relies almost entirely on its tech-savvy, company-integrated customer.

On the other hand, business start-ups that do not have the luxury of traditional revenue streams tend to create an entirely new offering. A noteworthy predominance of B2B business models within the examined start-up companies can be observed, whereas established businesses lean more towards a combination of both B2C and B2B. Over 80 per cent of the companies target business customers with their offerings (70% only B2B, and 13% both B2B and B2C). The vast majority of companies in the sample offer information or knowledge, which certainly relates to the selected sample. Web-based business models are predominant with start-ups on AngelList, and therefore most of the offerings are also Web-based. For example, the start-up Farm logs offers a service to farmers that streamlines crop and fertilizer input with satellite monitoring and weather and produces pricing patterns, increasing efficiencies throughout the farming process, thus enabling farmers to reduce unnecessary costs and improve practices and ultimately increasing revenues.

- **What data do we require and how are we going to acquire it?**

Data is obviously fundamental to a DDBM. Deciding which data is most applicable, and the nature of that data's acquisition, is pivotally important to the success of a DDBM construction. Established businesses with a substantial number of customers, and therefore potential customer interaction points, are well positioned to effectively utilize customer-provided data within their DDBM, although this data is often combined with data from other sources. Customer-provided and acquired data was utilized by 80 percent of the business organizations analyzed, with self-generated and existing data utilization slightly lower at 75 per cent. Free available data was the least exploited; with 60 per cent of the business organizations analyzed using this data source. This high utilization of all available data sources by established organizations is indicative that these organizations understand the value of data and orient themselves towards becoming data-driven. Telecommunications, retail and financial services consider self-generated data to be the most significant data source, with telecommunications and retail placing particular emphasis on self-generated data – probably due to their industry-specific customer interactions. Customer provided data is utilized and regarded as important across all of the analyzed sectors, which is suggestive of established business organizations viewing data as a source of leverage.

For example, the fashion retailer Top shop combines customer-provided data, free available data from fashion blogs and social media and existing data within its own databases when running predictive and descriptive analytics protocols to determine emerging trends within the highly competitive retail clothing industry. Without these processes in place to manage and capitalize upon the valuable source of potential customer insight, the available data, fashion retailers would lose out on significant revenue opportunities. Start-up companies have the advantage of a 'clean sheet' when constructing a DDBM, but also the disadvantage that they rarely have the luxury of a high number of recordable customer interaction points that can be utilized in their DDBM constructs. Instead they must depend primarily on external data sources. For example, the Web recruitment specialist Gild is a start-up that scours the Internet for talented Web developers using its evaluation software to analyze online coding, which is free and available to access. Once an innovative and skilled piece of coding has been identified Gild contacts the developer directly. By incorporating free available external data into its DDBM, Gild has created an effective way of identifying outstanding emerging talent for its recruitment process.

- **In what ways are we going to process and apply this data?**
Methods of processing reveal the true value contained within data. Knowing which key activities will be utilized to process data enables the business to plan accordingly, ensuring that the necessary hardware, software and employee skill sets are in place. To develop a complete picture of the key activities, the different activities were structured along the steps of the 'virtual value chain'. To gather data, a company can either generate the data itself internally or obtain the data from any external source (data acquisition). The generation can be done in various ways, either manually by internal staff, automatically through the use of sensors and tracking tools (e.g. Web-tracking scripts) or using crowd-sourcing

tools. Insight is generated through analytics, which can be subdivided into: descriptive analytics, analytics activities that explain the past; predictive analytics, which predict/forecast future outcome; and prescriptive analytics, which predict future outcome and suggest decisions. The analysis showed that analytics were regarded as the dominant key activity by both established businesses and business start-ups. Established businesses utilized all forms of analytics, whereas start ups predominantly favoured descriptive analytics and unspecified analytics. Predictive analytics (90%) was the most commonly utilized type of analytics, although descriptive analytics (80%) and prescriptive analytics (65%) were still utilized by a significant percentage of the businesses selected. The key activities of data acquisition and generation were practised by significantly more established businesses. This may be because established businesses are positioned within a marketplace in such a way that they can take advantage of these activities. Distribution was higher among business start-ups. This is linked to the subscription-fee revenue model option depicted in Figure 5. The inherent size of start-up businesses prescribes their tendency to present their company offering as a service requiring distribution with a subscription fee, whereas established businesses instead have a tendency to be more insular with their data and its uses to create value internally. The telecommunications sector has a varied range of key activities. Data generation and acquisition were the key activities with the highest percentage of references, each having 14 per cent. Unspecified analytics, descriptive analytics and prescriptive analytics were also regarded highly, each claiming between 11 and 12 percent of the reference percentage. Analytics in various forms were utilized consistently by the retail sector, with prescriptive, descriptive and predictive analytics each accounting for 12 to 14 per cent of all references and unspecified analytics accounting for over 20 percent. Data acquisition (12%) and processing (10%) were also regarded favourably as key activities by the retail sector. In the financial services sector, where finely-tuned predictive analytic modelling influences business decisions, Goldman Sachs plans years in advance to ensure it has the capacity, hardware, processes and employee skill sets available to utilize increased data volumes and new technologies. In fact approximately 30 per cent of all Goldman Sachs' employees work in technology and development. Descriptive analytics was the key activity, with the highest reference percentage in publishing at 24 percent. This was followed by predictive analytics at 17 per cent, data acquisition at 15.5 per cent and prescriptive analytics accounting for 14.5 per cent of the key activity references for the publishing industry. Retailers Zara and Top shop input both internal and external data sources into their system when running predictive and descriptive analytics protocols. The insurance sector's key activities within a DDBM are dominated by analytics, with over 75 per cent of all references aligning to at least one form of analytics. Data acquisition was of secondary importance, accounting for 9 per cent of the key activity references.

How are we going to monetize it?

Without the target of a quantifiable benefit to a business it is difficult to justify DDBM construction and implementation. Incorporating a revenue model into a DDBM is integral to its operational success. Seven revenue streams are identified by Hartmann et al (2014): asset sale, giving away the ownership rights of a good or service in exchange for money; lending/renting/leasing, temporarily granting someone the exclusive right to use an asset for a defined period of time; licensing, granting permission to use a protected intellectual property like a patent or copyright in exchange for a licensing fee; a usage fee is charged for the use of a particular service; a subscription fee is charged for the use of the service; a brokerage fee is charged for an intermediate service; or advertising. Revenue models associated with a DDBM differ considerably from a standard subscription fee such as The New York Times for advertising. These models vary considerably between sectors and within industries. Advertising is the revenue model utilized most by the established organizations analyzed, with 70 percent of the companies practising this revenue model. Usage fee was the second most commonly used revenue model among the analyzed business organizations, with 35 per cent utilizing this, followed by renting, lending and leasing (30%), asset sale (25%) and subscription fee (25%). With the exception of finance, each sector favours advertising as its dominant revenue model. In retail over 90 percent of revenue model references were for advertising, with 70 per cent in the insurance sector, 59 percent in telecommunications and over 50 per cent in publishing. In the finance sector, advertising references accounted for only 22 per cent of revenue model references, with the remaining 78 percent referencing lending, renting or leasing activities, which form the foundation of many business organizations in the finance industry. Other than advertising, the publishing sector showed a strong use of subscription fee as a secondary revenue model, with 32 per cent of references attributed to this activity.

The variation among revenue models is much more substantial within established businesses, although advertising is presented as the dominant revenue model. The Times is a good example of this. The current CEO realized that as physical readership continued to decline, thus reducing revenues, a unique aspect of the company was its access to a particularly high calibre of readership. With its online offering continuing to expand, it was decided that the company would offer its content online for free although its competitors charged their online readers. With no-cost access, online readers of The Times browsed the website freely and each click and article read logged and tied the individual user preferences through his or her account. Descriptive analytics allowed the Times to build a profile unique to each reader, enabling them to be targeted by advertisers both on and off The Times' website and charged at a premium because of the attractive demographic of the readers. The revenue model for business start-ups was dominated almost entirely by either usage fee or subscription fee. Welovroi, a start-up Web application that allows marketers to directly measure the effectiveness of digital marketing campaigns, offers its services to customers in exchange for a subscription fee. Business start-ups may be inclined to utilize a usage fee or a subscription in their DDBM revenue model, as it is a consistent payment and an effective way for a start-up to maintain liquid capital. The examples of The Times and Welovroi show how a business must become adaptive to the ever changing environment within which it sits. As current technologies improve and new technologies emerge, the effect on markets, industries and individual businesses are often unforeseen and difficult to predict. Through the use of industry-focused innovation platforms like the DDBM blueprint, businesses can assess their individual position and look to capitalize upon new and emerging business opportunities.

- **What are the barriers to us accomplishing our goal?**

Interestingly, our research and analysis revealed clear links between specific inhibitors to the implementation of a DDBM (based upon a qualitative survey targeting strategy) and data-oriented individuals (41 elite interviewees). In established businesses that strongly agreed they had personnel issues, 100 per cent also either strongly agreed (83%) or agreed (17%) to experiencing cultural issues when attempting to implement a DDBM. Furthermore, of the established businesses that strongly agreed they had personnel issues, 86 per cent also either strongly agreed or agreed to having internal value perception obstacles to implementing a DDBM, and 71 per cent agreed or disagreed to experiencing data quality or integrity issues. This analysis is suggestive that issues with personnel may be the most severe DDBM implementation inhibitors experienced by both new and established businesses and may be linked to a variety of other obstacles to a business becoming data-enabled. The data illustrated in Figure 6 suggests that if an established business organization does not have sufficient data-oriented and experienced personnel within its business then a company culture that is not conducive to constructing and implementing a DDBM is likely to emerge. This may also lead to the development of a negative perception of DDBM construction and implementation within the business. According to these findings, having or obtaining experienced data-oriented personnel who recognize and understand the fundamental principles and potential value of constructing and implementing a DDBM can reduce the effect of the most severe inhibitors to effective DDBM implementation. Training seminars to educate existing staff or similar instructional courses relating to the methods and benefits of DDBMs are among the tools a business may devise to reduce personnel resistance to becoming effective in applying new data-driven policies and procedures.

In today's fast - paced global economy, it is generally understood that companies must become data - driven in order to remain competitive. In fact, a report from McKinsey Global Institute indicates companies that are data -driven — meaning those that can gather, process, and analyze data in real- time as it flows through the enterprise — make better decisions. According to the report, being data -driven results in a 23x greater likelihood of customer acquisition, six times greater likelihood of customer retention, and a 19 x greater likelihood of profitability. But how exactly does a company become data -driven? There are, in fact, many ways to respond to this question. One might consider the use of technology or having a solid strategy for data quality, governance, and access, but perhaps the most important factor in becoming data - driven is having the right leadership to create a culture that places data at the heart of the organization. Change management is defined by CIO Magazine as" a systematic approach to dealing with change both from the perspective of an organization and the individual. " Instituting a culture around putting data at the core of every business function can be very useful in helping your employees and company understand and believe in the importance and use of data to make more informed decisions. Many of the senior IT leaders at my previous companies used the Kotter change management model developed byJohn P. Kotter, a widely- recognized authority on leadership and change, to bring about change in their organizations.

There are eight phases in Kotter's model and I want to detail how organizations can apply each to become more data driven themselves. In addition to the six vital answered questions here are some tips of establishing a data driven organisation.

1. **Create a Sense of Urgency**

This is one important, phase in Kotter's change management model can be used to demonstrate the benefits of becoming data - driven. The aim of this activity is to demonstrate to stakeholders how the company can use data for greater insights, underscoring some of the opportunity costs of not using data efficiently. This phase can be driven by a team of change agents comprised of senior execs who can tackle some of the organization's most important issues by using data. A simple business intelligence report showing some interesting insights around the various ways that customer service impacts sale could serve as an excellent example. Similarly, running an analysis showing where competitors are in their data journey on the maturity models and comparing that with the organization's own status in its data -driven transformation can also underscore the importance of data.

Build a Guiding Coalition

In this phase, the change agent needs a commitment from other leaders in the organization to drive the interest generated during phase one of the process. The bigger the change, the company, and more senior leaders are needed as part of the change team. While the change agent will need buy - in from business team senior leaders, IT will ultimately need to execute this portion of the strategy. Ideally, the members of these teams are drawn from the departments that will realize the greatest benefit from a data -driven strategy. For example, in a huge consumer products company, having leadership from the supply chain as part of the coalition would be a great win for the change agent.

Empowerment

As a data driven culture starts to develop within the organization, it is important to identify and tackle any obstacles head on. Leadership needs to ensure the right processes are in place that allows employees to raise concerns about how data is being leveraged and ensure those concerns are reviewed, considered, and addressed if changes do indeed need to be made. This activity also involves giving business workers the right tools that allow IT maintains governance and security over the data, such as self -service data preparation tools.

4. Generate Short-Term Wins

In this phase, a company's cultural change is maintained by savouring the success of winning projects and recognizing the efforts that led to that success. At the outset, a company can identify low -hanging fruit - projects that can be executed without much initial investment. These projects avoid the need for significant upfront monetary or staffing resources and provide the added benefit of shorter life cycles, allowing project managers to more easily define the specific goals and objectives that can help maintain momentum and foster a sense of accomplishment. As these projects become successful, leaders need to keep looking at other opportunities to make data an asset to the company.

Keep Track of Lessons Learned and Keep Looking Ahead

By keeping long term goals in mind and using some of the lessons learned from short term projects, a company can start implementing some longer term projects. For example, a company can invest in building a data warehouse and business intelligence (BI) capabilities within the company. A company can also invest in big data technologies and create a data science team. IT will also need to take an even more proactive role in the change management process by helping every employee within the organization understand the value of data quality and data governance. The company should also create more change agents by showcasing successful data -driven projects to other company departments.

Institutionalize Change

Clear communication can play a central role in demonstrating how the data - driven changes are directly related to performance improvements of the company. Leaders that champion the change should be placed in roles that allow them to drive the overall data enablement vision, such as a chief data officer (CDO), while other leaders take up new roles and responsibilities. The final stage in a data -driven transformation occurs when the changes become ingrained in the corporate the culture and that shift can then serve as the final platform on which the company can sustain the change. Leadership needs to embrace the fact that bringing about change within a company is a challenging and often long process. And that's the reason it is worthwhile to follow a framework such as the one outlined above, which suggests a phased approach and gives an opportunity to correct errors along the way and thereby realize the full potential of embracing big data.

Why Be Data-Driven?

Every company tries to provide value to their customers. The more value they provide to their customers, the more the value of the company goes up (at least in theory). But one may ask: How do you measure the value of a business? The financial industry has come up with various ways to measure the value of a business. Two of the most common financial measures that people look at are EV (Enterprise Value) and EBITDA (Earnings before Interest, Taxes, Depreciation, and Amortization). The ratio of EV/EBITDA is commonly used when comparing a firm's fiscal performance. The lower the value of the ratio, the more attractive your company is for private and individual investors. Alternatively, the best way to decrease the value of the fraction is by having a high EBITDA value. Calculating EBITDA for all non -financial purposes is the same as EBIT, which is revenue minus expenses. Therefore, the higher the revenues and lower the expenses, the higher the value of the business, which completely makes sense!

As the Federal government agencies begin the digital transformation journey, becoming a data -driven organization is even more vital. What does it mean to become a data -driven organization? According to one definition, " [a] data - driven company is an organization where every person who can use data to make better decisions, has access to the data they need when they need it . " There are many theories are on how to create a data -driven organization, but few case studies that demonstrate the actual process.

In this article, I will describe the results of four recent case studies that showed how a bank, a health care organization, a Fortune 500 company, and a municipal government became data driven.

Locating and Preparing the Data Assets

Locating and preparing data assets is the hard work of creating a data - driven organization. Consider the vast number of data sources in the average Federal agency. Where the data is located, how is it stored, what types of technology are needed to access and manipulate the data, and how to extract the dat. Agency data sources often grow organically which means there is a multitude of technologies that silo the data sources from each other? As I have found in gaining my data science certification, much of the data scientist's work is locating and cleaning the data to prepare it for analysis. Locating and preparing data assets can be the costliest and time- intensive task in creating the data - driven organization.

Establishing Data Partnerships

It is the rare organization where all the data resides in one office or department. Often, data sources are spread throughout the organization and subject to different departmental jurisdictions. Delicate negotiations must create data sharing partnerships and an enterprise -wide information governance. Data partnerships may also require going outside the organization to establish access to vital data sources. Creating and managing data partnerships will also take much time and can easily be derailed by even one or two dissenters.

Leadership Views Data as a Strategic Asset

Once the hard work of steps one and two are accomplished, being a data - driven organization requires ongoing senior leadership support. Senior leaders must champion the use of analytics to inform agency decisions and support the results of data analysis even if the analysis runs counter to the leadership ' s initial assumptions. Senior leaders also must support the governance of data assets and maintaining data partnerships.

Using Data for Organizational Innovation

The case studies demonstrated how the data -driven organization could commercialize its data assets. Commercialization of data assets does not apply Federal agencies. However, using data assets to create organizational innovations for the agencies is a promising area. Using analytics can help agencies redesign offices to take better advantage of existing agency talent to meet new strategic mission requirements. Analytics can also help agencies to develop new citizen services to meet public demand more effectively. Many models exist on how an organization can become data -driven. The four steps above are common to those models and demonstrate how the Federal government agencies can best use their data assets to transform the organization to serve the American public better. Each week, The Data Briefing showcases the latest federal data news and trends. Visit this blog every week to learn how data is transforming government and improving government services for the American people. If you have ideas for a topic or have questions about government data, please contact me via email. Dr. William Brantley is the Training Administrator for the U. S. Patent and Trademark Office's Global Intellectual Property Academy. You can find out more about his personal work in open data, analytics, and related topics at BillBrantley.com. All opinions are his own and do not reflect the opinions of the USPTO or GSA.

Challenges and Possible Solutions to Data-Driven Marketing

The new marketing mantra says, "Know your consumer and use this knowledge for good". It sounds as easy as that. However, there is a trick. We all understand that shoppers are getting smarter and increasingly less predictable - they use multiple channels throughout their shopping journey; they get information about the product from different sources, they may never even visit your shop in reality before making a purchase. You may never even see your real customer's face- to-face. Getting that "consumer data" has never been more challenging. Your customers expect you to know who they are, what keeps them up at night, what time they have breakfast at and which brand of soda they refer. Ok, that's a bit of exaggeration here, but it's true that consumers expect timely and relevant messages from marketers, otherwise they tag that ad, email or newsletter as "spam" and get rid of it without a single drop of remorse. And if they dump you once, don't even hope they will give you a second chance later. So, one conclusion to be made here: without a 360-degree view of your audience and precise analytics based on insights gathered both online and offline, don't even try to bother those people with your ads. For this reason, using data to shape a marketing campaign is not just a passing trend. Data- driven marketing is simply how it's going to be from now on, just get used to it. It's been an agreement among marketers worldwide that data not only matters, but it's considered to be the most precious asset of any organization, regardless of the industry or sector.

How to Make Data Work for You, Not Against You
Even though data may give quite a headache, marketers still realize that it's a necessary evil. If treated right, data can become your best friend, but if neglected your worst enemy.

Here are the top- notch industry ideas for an effective data driven marketing strategy:

Accept That Data Is Always Right, Not Your Gut Feeling
It may be painfully obvious, but since you're spending so much time gathering that valuable data, be careful not to throw it into the trash accidentally just because somebody else has a different opinion. Marketing is evolving fast, and someone might think he knows how things work, even if data suggests otherwise. This phenomenon is sometimes referred as "highest paid person's opinion", and it means that people tend to listen to the opinion of those who has the higher position in a company. It is crucial that every person in the office, from top to bottom, understands the power of data and starts making decisions based on hard numbers and facts, rather than making assumptions or reading the crystal ball. Send a clear message to the staff that no decision has to be made unless they are backed up with data.

Create A Data-Driven Corporate Culture

To become a truly data- driven organization, data must be shared among business units and departments and be managed consistently. For this reason, make sure your business adopted a strategic approach to data organization wide. Imagine just for a second that you need to create a targeted sales list. So you go a sales department and ask for customer information, then you go to product department to get data from them, then you compare it...it may take months! Furthermore, departments are not always willing to share information and you may wait for even more approval. If all departments operate as though they are on their own, there is no wonder why data become trapped within silos. A good data integration system would allow marketing department view information from multiple sources in a unified fashion. Customer data integration (CDI) gathers all data from disparate systems in various business units within an organization and assembles it in a single point, making it easily accessible. CDI allows an organization to gain deep customer insights and maintain customer data in real time. When you get your data in one place, it will be easier to merge it, standardize, transform and cleanse it, enhancing the effectiveness of business processes, reducing the risk and improving data privacy.

Store Data In One Place

For most companies, original data is treated as a top secret and used exclusively to drive business decisions inside one or two departments whereas others are kept in the dark. Data has to become more transparent and available for the team. Make sure everyone has access to the database and that they understand how to get insights from it. One way is to use an open data platform, which will allow using big data tools and integrate old data with the new. Open data platform may give business space for collaboration and opportunity to share data with the whole organization. However, be cautious not to turn that "data lake" into "data swamp", before pouring all data into one system, analyze your business needs and choose a problem where data could provide a tangible benefit. Invest in those cases first and then gradually, with the help of IT, move towards gaining mature analytical competency and complete data integration.

Obtain A 360-Degree View

If you rely solely on first- party data or the information you have collected about your audience, it won't get you too far. First- party data is still considered to be the most valuable because of its quality and safety. First-party data it' s information you have in your CRM, social data , subscription data , data from eligible benefit " behaviours or actions demonstrated across your website and so on. Yes, it is precisions, and it is indispensable, but to obtain the 360-degree view, you'd better use a third- party data and a second-party data as well. Third-party data is typically generated on other platforms and aggregated from other websites, and does not come from a direct relationship with consumers. This type of data enables deeper analytics of first -party data; appending these two allows building better consumer profiling and improves targeting for campaigns. Second-party data is a relatively new member of the family, which is basically the first -party data that you can get directly from the source. An exchange is always happening between trusted partners who are willing to share their customer data, making it beneficial for both parties. Therefore, there is no need to lock your data only for internal use; it may bring you more benefit if it is in circulation. The bottom- line is the more data sources you have, the clearer picture you obtain.

Do Something With Your Data

Ok, so you've been collecting gigabytes of information, from multiple sources, processing it day and night, organizing it into a single unified system...and now what? What shall you do with all that? As a data-driven marketer, your intuition tells you that it' s not just enough to gather data and report on it, it has to be put in use somehow. When you get tons of data on who your consumers are, what their interests are, what websites they visit, how much they spend on your webpage, the best thing you can do with this seemingly unrelated data is to offer a more personalized touch. How? For example, predict what customers would need before they ask for it. Recommended music on Sound Cloud or Spotify is all good examples of offering something that a customer might like based on his music preferences and audio history. One more thing you can do with your data - is to use it for improving customer relationships. By extracting data - rich info, the company's representative may react quicker and solve the problem more efficiently. For example, Pizza Hut knows that its customers are always concerned about pizza delivery time and delays due to traffic or weather conditions. Based on this insight, Pizza Hut implemented a GPS location tracking available across desktop, tablet and mobile so consumers can find out how close their pizza is an estimate the time of arrival.

Finally, don't be afraid to share your data with consumers! People absolutely love it. Because people are more and more concerned about how their personal data is being used by companies, data -driven content might become a great way to help companies build transparency and trust with consumers. Once people get hooked on their personal data, they would start using the product even more and be willing to share even more information with you. Big data is not the goal, but the method

With big data companies, you can get a better understanding of their customers, provide a better service for them and improve customer retention. However, it's not enough to collect consumer data and pile it up. Only with a detailed analysis, using various metrics, measuring immeasurable, companies can get most out of the raw data. Big data is only valuable if it is processed and interpreted.

The 3D Data-Driven Age

Decentralisation
Data created, stored and processed on a wider variety of systems, platforms and devices. Much of this data is in sources which fall outside core enterprise systems and platforms increasingly, much of the data is created outside internal IT platforms – Open Data, Social Media data et al. More organisational data held outside company boundaries on external Cloud based platforms.

Democratisation
Data-driven digitisation requires more data democracy; data must be accessible to all people who need it, when they need it. Self-service becomes the predominant model – users want to acquire, manipulate & use data, and do it for themselves.

Devolution

The IT Department no longer has monopoly control of data creation and storage,

It can no longer dictate all technology and must accept some degree of chaos.

Benefits Of Being A Data Driven Organisation

We use value to anchor the big data strategy. Big data allows us to create and protect values in ways that were not possible before. It helps organisations understand more comprehensively what drives customers, suppliers and employee's behaviour. It keeps focus on the value drivers that will have the greatest impact; therefore bets can be placed appropriately. For example, if for a fast food chain, one of the key value drivers is restaurant location and placement. Previously you would have tracked footfall traffic by physically fusing market surveys and counts. Now you can track mobile phone movement as well as other sources to understand where the best location is.

The outstanding speed in technology development has brought about effective change at an incredible rate. For example, in 2011 there were approximately 100 marketing science data analytics providers whereas at the start of 2014 there were over 1,000. This incredible growth is set to continue.

If you chase after technology without purpose, you will burn lots of money and not know where to focus. Having your organisation driven by data will help aversion of such misfortunes. No place for guesswork. if things are not transparently defined, we all know how different people interpret the same things differently. Without valid data, you will be resorting to guesswork and gut feeling. Sometimes you will be right and a lot of times you may be wrong. As a leader, people do expect you to be right, always! if you get it wrong then you will be seen as unfair or at the best incapable. And hence, the guesswork and the gut feelings must be avoided as much as possible in the data -driven culture. Better success for new initiatives one of the key reasons for the failure of the new initiatives is the lack of well- defined measurement. In a data-driven organization/culture, for any initiative, you first think about how that will get measured. This attitude itself provides a base for continuous improvement and hence the likelihood of success of the new initiatives becomes higher. The transparency in collecting and using the data ensure that people see the leaders as transparent. Furthermore, people know that things are transparent and in such case, they try their best to stay fair, which in turn improves fairness in the overall system. However, we do need to be careful in a certain aspect of transparency. Specifically, there is an age-old recommendation that "praises in public and criticizes in private". The transparency and data collection do need to ensure that these softer aspects are taken care. When this is done appropriately, it creates an amazing environment of trust.

Role model for others - the transparency and crowd sourcing ensure that people who are aligned and focussed on the company purpose gain more visibility. Of course, other people can drill down to see what is making them more successful and visible. This is where it is important that the feedback must be objective and it must exactly explain why someone is being appreciated. For example, if a company has one of the core values as "continuous improvement" and one of the employees shows visible improvement then it should be explicitly mentioned while appreciating the individual. This acts as a great reference and motivation for others as well.

Year-end arguments vs. daily improvement the traditional subjective system and hence culture was always giving way to a discussion like "why my friend is rated better than me, while we did similar work"? In the year end, this one discussion is so subjective that none is right or wrong and eventually a huge withdrawal happens. Both the parties compromise and in best case decide to move on with damaged energy level. With data - driven culture, the transparency ensures that people have ample opportunity to see what is going on around them and pick themselves up and be counted. They do see that they have more control on their success as they can stay focussed on their daily improvement.

Let's take for instance you have put the time into building a data-driven culture, your team is on the same page about metrics and goals, the data is transparent, and you have engaged a well robust software in place for proper data analysis. Just beating the drum around being a data- driven culture will not help. You seriously need to get down to using this to make things more effective for yourself and your organization. For example, one of our customers is using employee engagement score for the following purposes:

- Quarterly / half- yearly rewards and recognition
- Yearly appraisal
- Salary hike
- Promotions
- Employee loan review and approval
- Advance salary review and approval
- Bonus
- Variable pay

Conclusion

"Information is not communication." By now, the buzzword - fuelled explosion of "big data" has settled and established the new norm, and organizations in the know have been arm ping up their data analytics game to get ahead – and stay ahead – of the competition. Experts agree that the key to success in the Information Age is ensuring that your workplace promotes a data -driven culture. According to Information Week, the "data - driven" organization is a concept that not all executives understand. "Data- driven" is not the same as being generally "data - savvy," and it does not limit its usage to data scientists or the IT department. Even if you have a stellar IT staff, without utilizing data in business strategy, there is only so far that your team can go. Forbes quotes IBM Chief Executive, Ginni Rometty, stressing that "if [businesses] choose to ignore data analytics, they will not survive."With big data analytics platforms, data can easily be accessed by different departments in an organization, and this sharing assists in cross- departmental collaboration that results in richer insights. (And insights drive solutions, which then drive profits, and profits tend to make people pretty happy.) Embracing a data -driven culture means that any employee can look at data, see what information that data provides, and translate it to their teams. That is how information becomes communication. A recent article adds that with any employee being able to understand data reports, it empowers everyone to contribute confident ideas, "because they will have the data to support their thoughts." More on that later... Every single person you employ should understand what metrics are important to your company; knowing the what, why, and how of each indicator tracked. Metrics in data also confirms fact over opinions, bias, or guessing. If a team member proposes a new idea, great! But where is the research to back it up? Training employees to present data with their suggestions safeguards businesses by referencing fact and lowering risk in decision- making. Founder of Correlation One, Sham Mustafa, praises analytics for this advantage: "Data reduces uncertainty and drives better decisions, data is a part of the core business strategy." Incorporating big data into your business strategy and applying it to the sales funnel drives clearer choices. The article from Ladyboss supports faster fact-based decision- making, and adds that it actually will "improve their workforce cohesiveness" by reducing business related arguments. With data analytics put in place, using metrics to back up results, there is less reliance on instinctual judgement and more resolve placed in the facts.

What a sigh of relief! Less pressure on the organization and surer results. Another focus shouldn't come as a surprise to any business leader: to succeed, you need strategy. NG-Data says that with the embrace of the data - driven culture, "teams are more apt to seek out data to help fine-tune strategies and objectives and can take a more active role in measurement and analysis." So, utilizing data helps sustain strategy as well! Leaders need to develop clear strategies for implementing more data usage into the workplace and that data in turn will assure stronger stratagem to produce revenue. The Business Journal provides three practices for these strategies. I'll leave it to you to choose which mental image is preferred;

- Integrate multiple big data strategies. The most efficient companies leveraging big data today are merging strategies.

- Build a big data capability. Construct a team with different skills; IT, analysts, statisticians, business managers. This team needs to work as a unit for the data - centric culture to be implemented successfully.

- Create a big data policy. Policies regarding social media, compliance, security, and privacy, all being mindful of the user experience. Unlike traditional enterprises, data - driven organizations don't grow linearly, but exponentially. Just look at the spectacular growth of companies like Amazon and Google, who have built their entire business models around the exploration and exploitation of information. What these companies have in common is a data -centric approach that goes beyond operational excellence. This requires them to put data and analysis front and centre in everyday business processes, and to think beyond silos and even the company's own walls (literally and metaphorically) to build meaningful collaborations. "If workers lack direction and don't know what actions to take – or if the right processes aren't in place to enable employees to make improvements – data initiatives will stall." – Gallup Business Journal. Finally, this brings us to employees. It is the people that make the data - driven culture really happen. Organizations should be determined to educate their teams on what role data analytics are going to play in the workplace, and what tools they need to access the information that these analytics will reveal to them. Information Week's post states that data being held back from users "frustrates efforts to use data strategically," and the organization then suffers from internal fragmentation. While most leaders wish to avoid fragmentation, and integrate data into their companies, these enterprises that have not focused on education may find that their teams are "less technically savvy" and will face challenges adjusting to new practices. Paul Bertin says that when it comes to creating a data driven company culture, it "emerges from the people who make up your company, data does not drive the company, people are the drivers." Technology doesn't threaten employees, and a data- driven culture doesn't mean that your team comes second. It takes a partnership of people and analytics; the data -driven workplace uses reporting and analytics to underline their successes. Information is not communication. Information becomes communication, when your business blends analysis with people, instinct meets insight and sharper evaluations are executed and attained. Joshua Jones of Strategy Wise asserts that "to create an ecosystem in which data -driven culture thrives, you have to have a strong balance of strategy, IT, and statistics, all working in harmony." Statistics and strategy should merge in the sales funnel, and data is a tool to support suggestions from people. The data driven organization puts data and analytics front and centre in its business strategy and throughout all echelons. It differentiates itself from competition by making data -driven optimization part of daily operations. The Economist completed some key research on data driven organizations, Eleven percent of respondents state that, in comparison to peers, their organization makes "substantially" better use of data. But top- performing companies comprise more than a third of this group, demonstrating the connection between data driven decision-making and organizational performance. A Data Driven Organization is a cultural statement whereupon, People ask good questions, and challenge assumptions and have healthy debates on where to make improvements, investments, or other changes. Many people in the organization have the skills, access to data, and some expertise with BI tools to perform data discovery tasks and are successful extracting insights from data .Meetings kick off with a display, discussions, and dive into data first to help shape opinions and the dialogue around facts. Presentations reference their data sources - and these data sources are available to appropriate people in the organization to review, challenge, and conduct follow up analytics. The IT organization provides a defined set of data management and BI services to assist the organization in their discovery efforts. A defined business strategy helps people focus their data discovery efforts. There are already efforts to drive organizational changes, improve communications, and to get "bottoms up" contributions. Becoming "data driven" is a key, but not the only cultural priority. Efforts to leverage data in decision making has measurable results - improvements in operations, sales, new revenue generating products, happier customers, et al. Data is shared and leveraged across different businesses, organizations, and products. There is priority, demand, and hunger to address data quality issues, to integrate multiple data sources, to capture new types of data, and to leverage third party data to become smarter, faster, and more competitive.

While many companies rely on data every day to make decisions or to create a better customer experience, few treat it as a business asset. By establishing value and responsibility for the information, it makes it easier to measure – which makes up the emerging discipline called infonomics. This also helps organizations to address data gaps, keep information aligned with business strategy and maintain data quality so decisions are not made on bad data, by enabling employees at every level to use the right data at the right time, data can foster conclusive decision- making and becomes part of the companies' competitive advantage. By now, it should be clear that big data technologies — and IT in general — can be used not only to cut costs but also to find efficiencies in operations, finance, supply chain , customer service , and various business functions of the company. Additionally, it can be used to generate revenue growth, enter new markets, and become more valuable to Investors in various industries.

Hopefully, we have shown a clear relationship between the values of data, how it can be utilised and managed by the company. With this as a foundation, companies can confidently start investing in the data -driven transformation goals. Focus on beliefs and behaviour at the heart of a data-driven company is a data-driven culture with every employee involved. From the CEO to the security guard who swipes security badges, from a data analyst to the person who orders office supplies, all employees have a role. Companies who focus on both beliefs (vision and purpose) and behaviour (picture, plan and participation) will have the most success of reaching the data-centric Holy Grail

References
First San Francisco Partners – Steps to Becoming A Data Driven Organisation - https://www.firstsanfranciscopartners.com/wp-content/uploads/2017/06/5-step-data-driven-org-First-San-Francisco-Partners.pdf
The DDBM Innovation Blueprint – The 2015 March Paper - https://cambridgeservicealliance.eng.cam.ac.uk/resources/Downloads/Monthly%20Papers/2015MarchPaperTheDDBMInnovationBlueprint.pdf

- Becoming A Data Driven Organisation –Data Governance (IRM UK, May 2017) -
  https://globaldatastrategy.files.wordpress.com/2015/08/becoming-a-data-driven-organisation-data-governance_mdm_irm_uk_may2017.pdf
- Becoming An Analytics Driven Organization – EY
  https://www.ey.com/Publication/vwLUAssets/EY-global-becoming-an-analytics-driven-organization/$FILE/ey-global-becoming-an-analytics-driven-organization.pdf
- MGI - The Age of Analytics Full Report
  https://www.mckinsey.com/~/media/McKinsey/Business%20Functions/McKinsey%20Analytics/Our%20Insights/The%20age%20of%20analytics%20Competing%20in%20a%20data%20driven%20world/MGI-The-Age-of-Analytics-Full-report.ashx
- https://www.forbes.com
- https://www.inc.com
- https://programs.online,utica.edu
- https://barnraisersllc.com
- https://www.gartner.com
- https://e-commerce-blog.de
- https://www.signia-hearing.com
- https://www.sivantos.com

2018 © Mirko Peters
Publisher and printing: BoD – Norderstedt (Germany)
ISBN: 9783752886481